To Mary -
Celebrate the magic & our beautiful wild places!

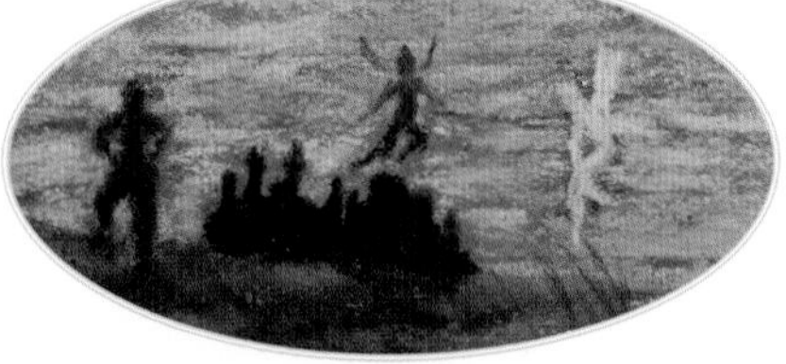

Look About You

A MAGICAL CHILDHOOD
IN MICHIGAN'S WILD PLACES

By
Erin Anderson

Erin Anderson

Artist
Mary Fuscaldo

Mary Fuscaldo
Enjoy!

Rimwalk Press

Cedar, Michigan

All inquiries should be addressed to Rimwalk Press
4249 S. Whitehill Drive, Cedar, MI 49621
E-mail: Rimwalkpress@aol.com

Library of Congress Cataloging and Publication Data
Anderson, Erin, author
Look About You
1. Title
ISBN 0-9720696-3-1   02-190006

First Edition
10 9 8 7 6 5 4 3 2 1

Printed in Hong Kong

To my father who has taught me,
by his own example, the true meaning
of service and stewardship.
— Erin Anderson

To Kalie who believes
and to Lauren and Lia
who someday just might.
— Mary Fuscaldo

If you seek a pleasant peninsula, look about you.
—*motto of the state of Michigan*

᠎

Once, when I was very young,
before the world could
teach me words like
"imaginary" and "make-believe,"
my father took my hand
and opened my world.

"There is more to life
than what we see," he told me,
"you must look deeper."

The places we went were not new to me.
I had seen them many times before.
But they had now become
whole new worlds
—empires unto themselves—
and I would never
see things in quite
the same way again.

᠎

Dead Stream Swamp

At Dead Stream Swamp we stood on the edge of solid land, our feet sinking into plants and earth ages old. The air hummed steadily with insects, so constant you could barely hear them at all.

There was such stillness, such quiet in the midday heat, that at first I thought he was only part of the tree, skin as weathered and bleached as wood, his face peeking from behind the trunk, eyebrows gnarled and arched as branches. He waited for us to leave, cautious, standing guard over the swamp like a sentinel, not lonely, but alone.

A bird flew in. His body nearly skimmed the water, his belly swept the grass. He circled longingly, looking for a welcoming roost, as if to ask the tree, "What is this place, this low wilderness moving in silence?"

Sleeping Bear Dunes

We climbed for what felt like miles, my short legs burning with the labored push of sand. My father's feet moved before me, soft rapids of wet earth tumbling from the soles of his shoes. With a strong arm, he pulled me into what seemed, at first, to be only sky. Here there were no trees but one or two standing silent in far-away gullies, no soil but sand the color of suntanned skin, and, further off, white, lying frozen like snow.

Then the wind picked up. Grasses moved like water, making the sound of waves, cutting great highways, thoroughfares, through the sand. I could feel something moving, could almost see it trudging determined, head bent to the blast, through these avenues of wind-swept life.

"These dunes," said my father as we scaled a small hill, "are more than just wind and sand. They are cover for a strong and essential life. Sometimes the greatest strength hides out in the open, where you least expect to see it."

Skegemog Swamp

nto a tunnel of cool, damp, dark we would descend, our bodies thankful for the release from summer's heat, our eyes blinking—confused—looking for the lost light. Slowly, we would adjust, raise our heads and gaze out from the entrance of sugar maples at the world opening slowly before us.

Once inside the forest, I clung close to my father's back, the wood seeming to open up, to expand its boundaries and tower above us, two small and slight figures beneath a dome so large you could not see its end. A part of me feared I would be left behind and lost. The trees were now spaced farther apart, tops reaching in leafy struggle for the sun. Down below there was little but trunks scraped silver in the half-light, ferns grown knee-high, and here and there a sapling, thin and pale, trying to take root.

The path wound on through the dimness, our feet sinking softly into moist beds of lichen and bark. My nose filled with the ancient, spicy smell of wood rot. My ears rang with the tiny sounds of a thousand things, each living their separate lives.

There was green so lush, so newly born, I felt I too must be the start of something rich and important, something just beginning.

In places sunshine lit our footsteps, surprising me, as though it did not belong—as though parts of the sky, pieces from another world, had fallen, scattered in golden shards on the forest floor.

After what seemed like hours, my father stopped, turned to scan our surroundings, then sat down upon an old, decaying beech log. I followed him down the leaf-lined gully and sat beside him, trying to avoid the sooty, peeling bark, the mulchy leaves sucking at my shoes. I rubbed my blackened palms on the legs of my jeans and looked at the soles of my sneakers in disgust.

Why was the woods so messy, I asked? Why was it covered in damp, dead things?

My father smiled, watched my eyes travel the hollows of that small valley, saw them light for a moment, squint, then look again. Something in the shadows moved, then stood silent—a figure tiny and gnarled, itself as old as the tree bark, the moss growing over its head.

"It is because of these dead things that we are here at all," he said. "We need them to fertilize new trees, new plants," he explained, reaching out his hand to rub a smudge from my cheek. "Everything that is old will one day begin anew."

The Frog Prince

Eight years old and you could not drag me indoors. I lived to breathe the outside air—to move effortlessly from one world to another with no walls to contain me.

While friends sat inside, watched endless hours of cartoons, played video games until their fingers were numb, I saw each moment as a doorway to discovery, as a chance to change my life.

Most people could not understand why I would want to get so dirty, climb so high, dig so deep, run so far and stay so long. I had no explanation—at least not one they would understand. Things others found useless and strange, I found vital and inviting. Although I could not say how, I knew that somehow these wild places made them feel afraid, made them feel small.

My aunt asked why I spent my days running through that filthy swamp, playing in that murky backwater.

They should fill that land, she said, save us from the mosquitoes and the stench.

One evening in May my father found me, sent to bring me in for supper. I had not moved all afternoon, sat staring from the cattails as streams of slick, green bullfrogs slid from the banks to swim through the shallow water, eyes skimming the surface like bulging, gold-rimmed periscopes.

We watched one particular frog, sleek sides puffing in the still, night air, his reflection a shining shadow beneath. I remembered a story my father had told me over and over, on those many nights when I could not fall asleep. I would imagine myself the lovely princess, picking the frog from the pond and placing it in the cupped palm of my hand. And each time my father told it, I would squirm, feel slightly afraid that this time, unlike all the others, the frog might not turn into the handsome prince. But he always did. And then I would sigh, heavy with relief, and sink slowly to sleep, the "moral of the story" sounding softly in the still room. "The frog was always the handsome prince underneath. Underneath is

what is truly important. He may not have looked like much, but once the princess truly came to know him inside, she was able to see his beauty shining on the outside too."

As we sat, watching the twilight linger on the lily pads, I realized that the story wasn't just about the frog prince, but about the whole pond, the whole swamp, all the wetlands in the world and everything else that did not shine with outward splendor. It all had a purpose far greater than its appearance let on. I asked my father why no one could see this place the way I did, why everyone told me I was wasting my time.

"People only value what they are close to," he said, "what they know and understand. These places are necessary," he reassured me. "Even those that, on the surface, seem useless. For instance, without this swamp we would not even have clean water to drink. These places are what keep us alive."

Showy Lady's Slippers

NEAR NORTHPORT

t a small clearing, deep within walls of cedar and pine, flowers stood so delicate and new, pink layered on pink, it seemed the air might crush them, and I was almost afraid to breathe.

"Whatever grows here will always be new, a miracle," my father said.

Suddenly, out of the corner of my eye, I thought I saw something move. A tiny bud, perhaps. Or maybe something more—something once dozing drowsy in soft greens, hair shining with dew, now waking like a flower.

Tree Spirits

When we set out on our walks to the woods, to begin our days together, my father's pace was anxious, his stride hurried, eager to get there, to begin our exploration. He wanted to follow the quickest route, to scurry along the busy road's narrow shoulder, secure that he was saving us both distance and time.

But I always lagged behind, dragged my feet, begged to take a different path, to make the journey part of our adventure too. For when you are ten you find friends in unexpected places and see brilliance where others find only ordinary existence.

My father stopped, then turned to face me on the road's bare, gravel edge. He smiled, "Alright," he said. "We'll take your way."

And so we took the long way to the forest, rambling miles off the quickest course, tramping through a meadow wide and endless as an ocean, my father forging

ahead through ferns dancing as light and wind-tossed as fragrant, green foam.

Fronds rustled in the breeze, spoke music to our bodies as they touched each curling leaf. Ahead I could see my tree, the meadow's only hardwood, standing tall and drying in the sun, bark bleached gray as ash, leaves so near the sky, so far away as to be almost forgotten.

As we passed, we peered at the split in its trunk, the hollow worn smooth by the years since whatever caused that wound.

It was then he saw it too. I could tell by his slowed step, his wide, smiling eyes. Two faces watched from the tree, silent, observing: two friends I had met long ago. No time to talk today. Maybe another—sometime soon. I was not worried. I knew they would be there when I returned. They always were.

Nearing the edge of the field, my father stopped, the woods standing dark green guard before us. "It was you who taught me something today." He reached for my hand to help me through the bordering branches. "I was so concerned with 'getting there' I nearly forgot the most important thing, and you reminded me. Never close your eyes to what's along the way. Remember, you must always look about you."

Faery Ring

Our steps took us miles from the house, through grasses dried the color of a sunrise. Ahead, hidden behind the deep cool of elm and wild pear, two buildings sat silent — a house and barn weathered gray and red, born it seemed from wild carrot and goldenrod. We walked to the glassless windows, placing our faces near the rough and splintered sills, those frames the ancient lids of vacant, staring eyes.

Inside, air heavy with the weight of loss circled the crumbling room—the chair overturned in the entryway, the poker rusted on the mantle, a tin pail in the corner—leaving, finally, it passed our faces, blowing cold and damp through my hair. What life had pulsed in the veins of that hollowed house? What dreams had been cradled in its strong and stony foundation?

My mind flipped freely through pictures of families, young children, quiet evenings in the indoor warmth of winter, family deaths, and fall harvests.

"What do you think they were like," I asked, "the people who once lived here?"

"They were possibilities, chances, maybes," my father said. "They were like every one of us."

We turned then to the field, the grasses brushing our legs hip high, the sun hot on the tops of our heads. Suddenly the grass fell away, lay trampled smooth in a dark circle against the earth.

"We can never fully know the past," he said, kneeling to stroke the glossy ring, "we can only see the mark it leaves behind."

It was then I heard a song, felt a movement in the air.
"Can you see us?" it asked, voice light, circling the ring.
"We dance in the shadows of what might have been."

Boardman River Sprite

I was twelve years old and had no place to think, no space to release my thoughts. The summer had been filled with change, chaos, and destruction. Orchards were uprooted, forests razed, old landscapes transformed—unknown objects lurking on a horizon I did not know. House after house appeared, buildings never ending. There seemed to be no room to breathe. What was once familiar, as much a part of who I was as where I was, was gone, replaced by a new and foreign nothingness people spoke of as "progress," as though the word was a thing in itself.

I felt I had been torn in two, the fusion of person and place rent with the sound of backhoes, chainsaws, and the stench of diesel fumes.

And so I took refuge in the river that summer, found solace in a valley of untouched land, the din of "progress"

hushed by the rustle of ancient pine, the whisper of water.

My father showed me a place removed, unchanged in years, protected by man's law from his own hands. Some days he would sit with me, our bodies cushioned by moss, held in the craggy comfort of cedar roots—a quiet cave from which to watch the water run, moving ever forward, then winding back again—the route unaltered in so many seasons.

It was one of these days when, as the daylight began to wane, I turned and saw a figure, small and dark against the remaining daylight, leaping lightly between the trees, as though it were dancing. As I looked closer, I realized how long it had been since I had seen one of these friendly spirits. The commotion of the summer must have driven them away from their old haunts, must

have sent them searching for a place they could feel at home, even as their true homes were being destroyed.

I asked my father then why it was said that "progress" should not be stopped.

"They're right," he said, his eyes following the journey of the river. "Real progress is a going forward, while also protecting what we leave behind. So it is for you to decide if all this is really 'progress' at all—what 'progress' really is."

Boat Houses

Rain in summer was like a sky-dashed dream, both earth and air gone gray. Often my father and I would be caught unaware in the sudden storms, halted, mid-step, our faces raised to the vanishing sun.

A thick morning in July we left the house early to follow the river, our pockets filled with breadcrumbs, fish hooks, jars of insects. My father walked ahead, his steps a song in the thick grass, the pliant blades brushing one another with an ecstatic hum. His footprints disappeared almost instantly from the live earth, the dark mud of the bank eager to fill the sudden, empty spaces. I felt the thunder first in my feet, the ground shaking with the rich reverberation. It traveled upward then, and out, finally reaching the tips of my fingers, the boundary of my skin, and here met the falling rain. The first drops came warm

and full, opening in slow, expansive splashes. All seemed to meld, to blur in an atmosphere of cloud and mist. Colors hid, took refuge from the storm.

My father stopped, turned around, "Do you want to go back?" he asked.

"No," I answered. "Let's keep going."

Ahead, nearly a mile down river, we saw the low frame of an abandoned boathouse, its worn wooden sides sagging with the weight of water. As we walked closer I could see, through the rain, a gathering of gulls on the roof. They sat calm and undisturbed, lulled by the straight and windless rain. For a moment I was sure I saw a tiny, bearded man among them.

Once inside we removed soaked shoes, wrung dripping socks steeped in wet. The afternoon passed at the window, the river a foggy mirror below, swallowing the storm.

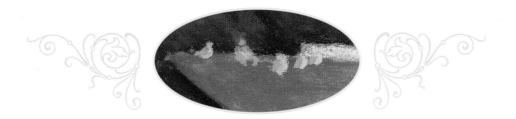

"I knew it would rain," my father said. "See how the whole world welcomes this drink."

Drops sounded hard on the roof, an unrelenting rhythm—crisp, constant beats. And between these notes, something warm, living, the carefree tapping of jubilant heels.

Old Mission Vineyard

In late summer, just before school began again, everything seemed to stop, time hovering like haze over the still ground. In the afternoon we walked to the vineyards, the dark, green leaves spilling over their trellises as if reaching, once more, for the comfort of the earth. At first I could see only green, the vines rolling downhill to the languid orchards, and in the distance the smooth blue of the lake.

"Look here," my father said, kneeling as he softly revealed the underside of the leaves. It was then I saw the fruit, hanging rich and swollen from nearly every vine, no two pieces the same, each grape a new meaning for the words blue, purple, and red. I was surprised when, from the stillness, I felt a movement in the vines, a current of energy shooting electric through these circuits, as if something had suddenly rushed, startled, from this cover.

The air held all summer in its gauzy hand, taut and full to bursting with a season's growth. But, it would wait a while longer before the letting go. It was not yet ready to turn to fall.

Enchanted Forest

id-summer spread slow and thick through my thirteen-year-old days. Mornings dawned clear and bright, changing in what seemed an instant to a heat-worn haze. By noon I would feel tired, weighted down.

"Come on," urged my father. "Let's go someplace else."

We walked through fields baked brown in the heat, our steps a hurried crunch, holding our breath for the cool of the wood. Once beneath the boughs we would relax, the calm quiet of the trees surrounding us, forming to our bodies like a worn, green glove. I inhaled deeply, filling my lungs with the life of maple and beech. The worries of those in-between-school days, of friends and finding my place, fell away as we wound along trails of startling quiet and stillness. The breeze blew high about our heads, branches tossing irreverent against the sun.

For a moment, the canopy broke, leaves separating to form a tunnel for the light.

I stopped in my path, reaching to touch my father's sleeve. He turned, following the point of my finger toward something spinning suspended among the forest's browns and greens. A whirling mass of energy, a shining chrysalis, it seemed to dance above the mushroomed ground, between the slick silver bark of a beech and an unsure spindle of red oak—between old and new.

"We will never lose this place," my father said to me, "it has finally been protected."

"I think it knows," I said, unable to explain my joy.

"You are right," he said. "See how everything has gathered to celebrate."

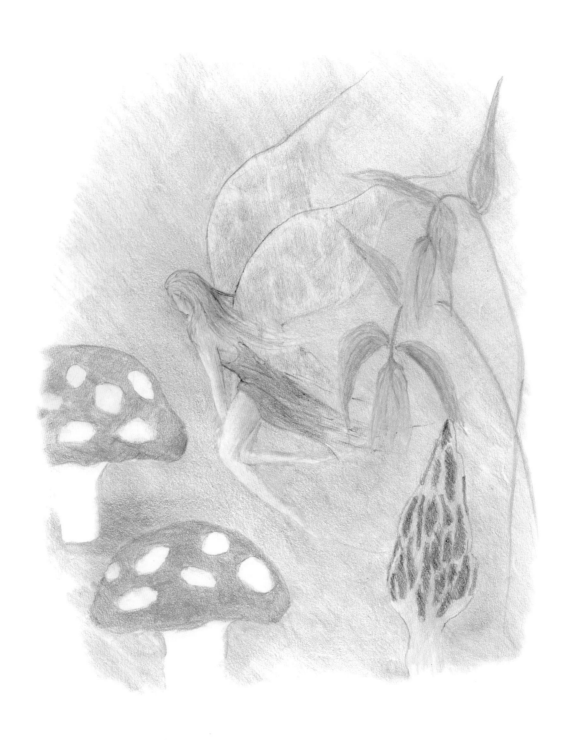

Approaching Storm

We walked in circles to the sky, our feet echoing on the ancient staircase like metallic heartbeats.

Nearing the top I could almost feel the urgency of the long-ago keeper, alarmed with the persistence of dusk, bounding anxiously over steps, some two at a time, forever upward, to light the lamp.

In the darkness that flame would be diffused, broken into thousands of misshapen pieces, and then restored, concentrated, absorbed into the hulls of hundreds of ships, each one navigating the bottomless black; a wanderer praying for dawn.

"You see?" my father asked, bending to take a piece of the shattered lens in his hand and holding it,

reverently, to the sun. I could. In that glass I could see the whole deep quiet of the island, the curve of the white-beached shore and beyond; behind, a stretch unbroken of cedar and pine. The only interruption, the only distur-bance in this endless peace: a small set of footprints, winding their way toward us through the brush. And this view was only a fragment, one piece of a dazzling whole.

I wanted to stay, to keep looking, to see all that the lens had seen—that great eye, open to both sun and storm.

That evening, leaving by water, I watched the tower slipping away in the shadows of that shore—dark—but, for a moment, lit bright by a blazing beam, the work of an unknown, but faithful, keeper.

Port Oneida Road

LEELANAU COUNTY

That year I heard the word "spring" spoken with color soaked in every sound. Year after year I had straddled that line—hazy and indistinct—between warmth and heat, beginning and middle, summer and spring. I had walked unknowing through that space between two seasons, unaware of its fullness, its capacity to make things whole.

Now, at fourteen, I suddenly woke to my father's words, suddenly watched amazed in the blurred beauty of that late May afternoon, my mind emptied of all thoughts beyond leaf, sun, and sky. I no longer could remember what, only a moment before, had seemed so important, had seemed to shape my very existence.

We left our house just as the sun began to slant, to lean, ever so slightly, back toward its bed in the earth. We walked for miles, our bodies parting a thin wake through meadows otherwise unbroken. The grasses stretched on,

their waving rhythm unending. We followed their new, silken stems along the gradual, soft slope of Five Mile Hill, my father leading the way—arms stretched out at his sides, palms open and turned down toward the earth. The young, tender tips sprung back from his touch—two rivers of motion flowing backward from his hands.

Reaching the crest of the hill he stopped, his body still slightly bent as though he were straining to continue that motion—up and up. In front of us lay a young field, new greens both light and dark relieved by reds, pinks, and whites. The brightness of poppies was a surprise to our unaccustomed eyes.

I too stopped short, looking beyond my father, beyond the mixed and wild field to the smooth, mown lawn, gravel drive raked even, the white house—its windows sleek and shining, throwing back the sun.

"I did not expect this," I told my father, feeling somehow disappointed, almost hurt that our solitary outing had ended, that the calm current of grass and sunlight had been broken with signs of someone else's life. I struggled to find words to explain this to my father.

"You know," he said, his hand sweeping back to our undisturbed path, then forward to include the flowers, the house, "every time humans meet nature need not be bad. Remember, just look about you." He turned around, then spun a full circle, his face, his eyes taking everything in. "Both must have a place to live, to breathe. The secret is finding a balance."

He turned then from the house, his hand a hood above his eyes, a shield from the brilliant sun.

That is spring, I thought. One must complement—feed—the other. Perfect balance. Within its precious days it finds room for all things.

Dawn Over Lake Leelanau

In late spring the coming dawn drew us from our beds, roused our bodies with the promise of its colors, woke our senses with the assurance of its light.

We would leave the closed comfort of our house in the pregnant dark—the others still sleeping—our steps shuffling silently over the floor, anxious for the freedom of daybreak.

We walked with the night, our movements quiet and quick—the path sunk deep in predawn black, our feet moving instinctually, knowing the way.

Reaching the bluff we stood still, overlooking the lake. We waited, watching as the air around us lifted, lightened somehow.

Suddenly a brilliant strip of light appeared—a pulsating gash of pink splitting the night in two. In an instant

the sky became separate from the blue-black hills, and from that deep rose glow the coming day spilled forth possibility.

With this lighted warmth came dew—the damp gathering on grass and shrub, dripping diamonds of moisture through our pant legs and onto our shoes.

And so I spent years learning how the world wakes, understanding the earth one morning at a time. I grew up in the spaces between dark and light, night and day.

Everything was so new and cool and untouched. It felt as though the air had not ever been breathed. Standing there that moment, it was as if we were the only people on earth.

"That is what the dawn is," said my father, widening his eyes to memorize the morning. "It's a chance to start over, for all things to begin anew."

Stone Arch

I slands are made of magic. That's what I discovered early one October, just before the first fall rains came and I turned fifteen.

We woke early, left the house in the pre-dawn dark to cross the waters in tight shivering silence, our bodies pulled inward on ourselves, nearly disappearing in the warmth of our coats.

For months I had stayed indoors, watched television, read one magazine after another—each promising to sell me the secret to things like flawless skin, perfect hair, how to impress certain boys.

I no longer went for walks with my father. So when he asked me to come with him now, I could not say no. As I stepped to the shore, I felt myself surrounded by silence and I was glad I had come.

I fell easily in line behind my father, my steps effortless, my feet moving as though in a dream. I did not

ask where we were going. I only wanted to be moving through this world of deepest color and shade. In this world removed, reds ran deeper, browns beat in time with the earth, and yellows crept closer to the sun.

I could feel we were wrapped within a place where nature still lived deeply, deliberately, far from the distractions, the complications, of the rest of the world. Life here was cleaner, brighter.

As we climbed farther into the blue, rocks tumbling beneath our feet, I began to see movement, first from the corner of my eye—a slight flicker of light—then growing, gaining both form and sound. I saw figures all around me—in the rustle of the leaves, the crunch of the rocky path, the lap of the lake far down below, at the shore.

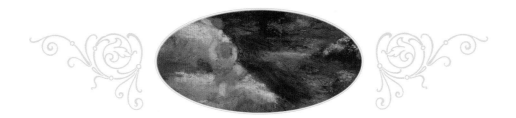

Nearing the great stone arch it was as though the world had converged, had focused all its energy on this place, had made this tiny island the keeper of its essence.

My father paused in his path, turned to see my wondering face, eyes widened with what I thought had been lost and was found again. "It's all still here," he said, seeing my surprise. "Sometimes you must remove yourself from your everyday life in order to be reminded."

Snowy River

Upper Peninsula

February—and no one around for miles, my father's and my footsteps the only interruption, frozen still under snow.

Waking that morning was no gentle journey, no cushioned free-fall into consciousness. Instead, it was instant awareness, my eyes burning with the brilliance of winter's colorless sun, its light reflected in each keen crystal of ice, in every flake of snow. My mind was already moving, racing beyond my window and out into that untouched, white world.

We dressed quickly, strapping on our snowshoes with clumsy, wooden fingers already bleached white in the raw morning air. We turned and headed toward the frozen silence of the river, its warm speech now suspended with the cold. Behind us, our snowshoes left tracks the shape of giant tears; an impatient spring's sobbing, suppressed only by the beauty of snow and stillness.

Our path sloped to the wood, winding through the sudden darkness of maple and pine. Each step rang crisp and clear, the sound moving quickly from snow to branch to treetop to air. Then the ground began to rise and on we climbed. It seemed as though everything had paused—stopped briefly in the midst of the earth's unending rotation to sit perfectly still and let the snow cover things both big and small, making equals of everything it touched, the foundation for a new and unspoiled beginning.

When we reached the crest of the hill, my father stopped short, his chest heaving beneath the thick layers of his coat, steam swirling from his nose and mouth. Below us lay the riverbed, the valley opening wide and flat between its borders of cedar and spruce. Here and there the ice had broken, the snow-covered surface part-ed to reveal water blue-black as ink. It seemed to stand silent, the current arrested mid-flow. The only movement

was the light pulsing not on, but rather within, every surface, as though the sun had lodged forever deep within the earth. Still, I could not turn away or shield my eyes. I too was frozen, in a trance.

"That," my father said, his gloved hand sweeping an arc over the valley. "That is the world mid-breath—resting—waiting for the moment to wake." He took one step forward, his right arm curling around a gray, towering trunk. We both stood silent, watching winter's heart pulse and shift with the ice.

Cathead Bay

There are some legends that never leave us, that enter us at such a young age we are completely unaware, and it is not until we wake one day and realize that we are nearly grown, that we know that these are what built our bodies and nourished our blood.

My whole life I had heard my father spin stories like gold, tell tales that took the mind so far through time you could not be sure where you stopped and the legend began. But by the summer I turned eighteen, I had forgotten how to hear. My father's words were lost in long lists of things I thought were more important: friends, parties, college plans. I could feel myself pulling away from my family. I was now grown up, I thought, and ready to go.

And then, in early August, a month before I left for school, my father came and took me back out into our world saying, "I think there's something you should see."

We passed though cedars, boughs hanging thick and heavy, branches folded down behind us, green and impenetrable, overlapping one another like dark, fragrant wings.

"Remember this place?" my father asked me.

And of course I did. Once again the world seemed to open within that sacred space; branches moving up the farther we moved in until, at last, the trees were merely pillars, columns of support, the leaves a vast, living ceiling overhead.

I could see those whose lungs had breathed that clear, cool air, whose feet had trampled that path from mere dust to near stone. I could hear their voices vibrate with music, their souls swell with song. Their whole history was here: their births, their deaths, their collective memory of who they were, all within this temple filled with the light of a thousand years.

"There were people here before us," my father said. "And after us, there will be others again."

And suddenly I no longer felt old, accomplished, ready to move on. Instead, I felt so small I could not remember why I had ever thought my own problems, my own life, so serious at all.

The smell of cedar spiced the ancient air. Outside the waves broke bare on the beach. There was a presence so real and so deep I did not move for fear that it would fade.

"Can you hear that?" my father asked, reaching out with a light hand on my shoulder.

And that's when I was aware, for the first time, of the destruction in the distance. Bulldozers and backhoes ground and churned to take the earth and swallow her whole. I could feel the spirit fading, receding into the shadows as though seeking shelter from a storm it knew it could not escape. I knew then that I did not want it all to change. I wanted some things to always stay the same.

"You cannot avoid change," my father said, turning to take a last look around him.

"We cannot change the fact that one culture comes after another, crosses oceans and borders to claim something that is not theirs, that people will always want to expand, to move, to have "more." We cannot change this any more than the fact that children will simply grow up and need to be on their own. There is much in life that is difficult, that hurts, but what matters is how we respond, how we right the wrongs; what we do to make these things balanced and bearable. These are the things we can control, the parts of our lives that we own."

To My Child, on the day you are born —

For nine months now you have been forming, slowly, bit by bit, your very being opening from the tightly curled bud of your own potential, opening like a flower.

I have been told by many experienced sources that the best gift that I could give you would be practical, something set aside and stored wisely, in the proper place, to sustain you later — money or jewelry or government bonds. But I have chosen another gift, decided to give the ramblings and remembrances collected in this volume, and I hope you will understand.

As I look out at what sun is left, cradled on the water's soft shoulder, I wonder if you will ever reflect on the memories recorded here and know through them, because of them, truths which cannot be directly spoken. And I think you will, for through me, you were present at them all and a bit of each is embedded in your skin, woven in every whisper of your breath, sewn in every smile.

As you grow, people will try to tell you that magic does not exist, that the world relies on the reality of a three-dimensional plane. Therefore, my great wish for you, my little one, is that

you will see beyond this and see further into a realm of infinite layers and levels, to a world wrapped and wound with limitless strands and strains of magic.

When I was younger, I saw this magic as a multitude of fairies shining in even the most remote recesses of the world. The light of their laughter, the whisper of their wings, it all spoke to me without words, of another world—a world running beneath ours on the slow and steady current of the earth's own time. It was not until years later, after trying to deny their existence, trying desperately to abandon all other senses in favor of pure "sight," that I learned to see them once again, only now more clearly. Now I do not only see them, but I feel them and I know them, everywhere. And this is because I now know they are here to represent the spirit and the story of each and every place. Our duty is not to overpower, to contain, or control this spirit, but to embrace and enhance it by the balance of our needs with its own. There is a common thread to both the earth's life and ours, if we will only look about us and listen; a common beat to our blood.

I do not wish to write anything I am not sure of, so I have written all that I know today—right now. And I know that today you are nothing but perfect possibility. I cannot wait to watch you open to the world, to show you these places that formed me and made me myself, to wonder at where the wind will take you. But you will discover your own dreams too, create connections within your own wild places. And, as this happens, these same spirits will be waiting for you, to show you what is strong and true in both your heart and the world's, from your first dance to your last.

All my love,
Your Mother

Rimwalk Press will contribute a portion of every sale
to the following conservancies:

The **Grand Traverse Regional Land Conservancy**
works to protect in perpetuity unique lands that provide
crucial wildlife habitat, preserve critical wetlands, main-
tain pristine shorelines and rivers, protect inland lakes
and watersheds, and save our unique farmlands. The
Conservancy is committed to protecting land using
methods that respect private property rights, that balance the needs of local communities, and that guarantee
the permanent protection of significant landscapes in
Antrim, Benzie, Grand Traverse, Kalkaska and
Manistee counties in northwest lower Michigan.

Grand Traverse Regional Land Conservancy
3860 N. Long Lake Road, Traverse City, MI 49684
(231) 929-7911 • E-mail:info@gtrlc.org

The **Leelanau Conservancy** was founded in
1988 by a group of dedicated residents concerned about impending development and its
impact on the beautiful Leelanau peninsula.
It's mission: "To conserve the land, water and
scenic character of Leelanau County." Since
its inception, the organization has earned a
reputation as one of the premier land trusts in
the country. The Conservancy has since protected land and touched lives
each of Leelanau's eleven townships. The conservancy accomplishes its
goals by means of purchases or gifts of land, conservation easements, water
quality monitoring and environmental education.

Leelanau Conservancy
PO Box 1007, Leland, MI 49654
231) 256-9665 • E-mail:: conservancy@leelanau.com

The **Little Traverse Conservancy** is a non-profit conservation organization working to protect the natural diversity and beauty of Northern Michigan. The Conservancy has created more than 125 nature preserves in the North and provides environmental education programs to thousands of children each year. Formed in 1972, the Conservancy has worked with landowners to protect more than 17,000 acres, or 25 square miles of natural and scenic land in Northern Michigan. This includes more than 58 miles of lake and stream frontage that has been premanently protected for generations to enjoy.

Little Traverse Conservancy
3264 Powell Road, Harbor Springs, MI 49740
(231) 347-0991 • E-mail: ltc@landtrust.org

Original paintings in this book done in soft pastel
on archival Pastelbord by Mary Fuscaldo.

Design by Angela Saxon,
Saxon Design Inc., Traverse City, MI